The Greatest Treasure

By Gillian Leggat

Kingdom Publishers

The Greatest Treasure

Copyright © Gillian Leggat

All rights reserved. No part of this book may be reproduced in any form by photocopying or any electronic or mechanical means, including information storage or retrieval systems, without permission in writing from both the copyright owner and the publisher of the book. The right of Gillian Leggat to be identified as the author of this work has been asserted by him/her in accordance with the Copyright, Designs and Patents Act 1988 and any subsequent amendments thereto.

A catalogue record for this book is available from the British Library

ISBN: 978-0-9935959-6-7

www.kingdompublishers.co.uk

1st Edition by Kingdom Publishers

Kingdom Publishers

London, UK.

Dedication

I would like to dedicate this book to Jennie, Robert and Susan

Gillian Leggat

"It will be like the pot of gold at the end of the rainbow," said Josh.

"Or a beautiful, shiny white pearl," said Sasha.

"No, I think it will be like a river, with fruit trees on either side," said Mary.

"But how do you get there?" asked Josh.

"Yes, is the journey hard?" asked Sasha. "Can we all get there?"

"Let me tell you a story," said the wise old woman.

So all the children went to sit in the shade of the massive oak tree to listen to the old woman's story.

There was once a tall, fair-haired boy called Sam who lived in a small town called Rainbow. In the same town lived Mr Bright. Every afternoon, this old man sat on his bench in the park, telling everyone who passed by about this fabulous treasure beyond their wildest dreams. But nobody in Rainbow town believed in this treasure. They all thought he was talking nonsense – except for Sam. He wanted this treasure for himself.

So one afternoon, Sam went to the old man in the park and said, "Have you really seen this fabulous treasure, Mr Bright?"

The old man's eyes glowed with a sudden fire. "Oh yes," he said softly, clasping his hands to his heart.

"Why's nobody else seen it except for you then?" asked Sam, putting his hand over his mouth. He hadn't meant to sound so cross.

"That's because they're not looking in the right place," chuckled the old man.

He waited a while, then he said, "Anybody who wants this treasure can have it."

"Anybody? Even me?" said Sam.

"Anybody. Even you," echoed Mr Bright, nodding his head like a wise old sage.

"Then tell me where I can find it," said Sam, stamping his foot angrily.

The old man looked at him calmly. With a mischievous twinkle in his eye, he said, "The treasure is closer than you think."

That made Sam even angrier. "How can I find this treasure when I don't know where it is or what I'm supposed to be looking for?" he complained.

To Sam's great disgust, the old man's head suddenly dropped onto his chest. In one minute flat, he was sound asleep! Sam was so fuming that he wanted to shake the old man awake. But he didn't dare. By now, a lot of young

children had come into the park. Well, he would just have to find this treasure by himself! A pity he lived in such a small town. Who ever lived in a town called – RAINBOW!

That was it. Now he knew exactly where to find his treasure. His very own pot of gold. At the end of the rainbow. He had read stories about people trying to find this treasure. But nobody ever had. He, Sam, who lived in the town called Rainbow, was going to be the one to find it.

Sam knew that for rainbows to appear in the sky it had to rain. So he waited patiently for rain. He waited a whole week. Then he waited another two weeks before there was a decent sized rainbow in the sky. Then, with sandwiches and water in his backpack, he set off to find his very own pot of gold. He hurried to the end of the road which led out of town, but by the time he got there, the rainbow had disappeared. He was hot and bothered, but even though he had come prepared, he didn't feel like eating or drinking now. He had to find Mr Bright. The old man simply had to tell him the secret of the fabulous treasure. He would shake it out of him.

So Sam ran all the way to the park, sprinting towards the old man's bench.

"Mr Bright, Mr Bright," he shouted, "tell me right now. Where can I find this fabulous treasure?"

The old man looked up, startled. He placed his chin in the palm of his hand, then, with the biggest smile on his face, he sang in a deep, musical voice, "You find this fabulous treasure right inside yourself."

Sam was confused. "But how..."

"You want a richer treasure than all the gold and all the rubies in the world? A pearl of great price?"

"Yes, yes," replied Sam, with great excitement.

"Ask Jesus into your heart and you will have the greatest treasure of all."

Sam's mouth dropped open. He was about to say something, but then he changed his mind. Instead, he opened his backpack, took out his sandwiches and water, and handed them to Mr Bright.

The Greatest Treasure

The Greatest Treasure

The Greatest Treasure

The Greatest Treasure

www.ingramcontent.com/pod-product-compliance
Lightning Source LLC
Chambersburg PA
CBHW050451010526
44118CB00013B/1786